THE DIAGRAM GROUP

FREAKY FACTS

STERLING PUBLISHING CO., INC.
NEW YORK

Library of Congress Cataloging-in-Publication Data Available

1   3   5   7   9   10   8   6   4   2

Published by Sterling Publishing Company, Inc.
387 Park Avenue South, New York, N.Y. 10016
A Diagram Book first created by Diagram Visual Information Limited
195 Kentish Town Road, London NW5 8SY, England
© 1996 by Diagram Visual Limited
Distributed in Canada by Sterling Publishing
% Canadian Manda Group, One Atlantic Avenue, Suite 105
Toronto, Ontario, Canada M6K 3E7
Distributed in Australia by Capricorn Link (Australia) Pty Ltd.
P.O. Box 6651, Baulkham Hills, Business Centre, NSW 2153, Australia
Manufactured in the United States of America

Sterling ISBN 0-8069-8127-X

When a honeybee finds a flower with plenty of nectar, it drinks the nectar and then flies back to its hive. There it does a special little "dance" to tell the other bees where to find the nectar.

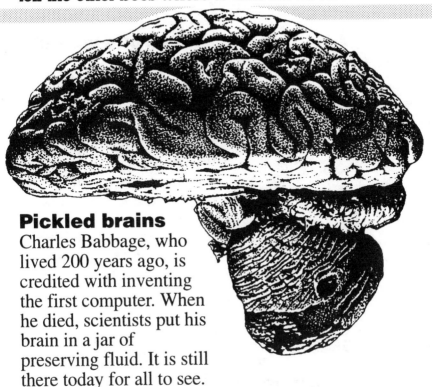

Pickled brains

Charles Babbage, who lived 200 years ago, is credited with inventing the first computer. When he died, scientists put his brain in a jar of preserving fluid. It is still there today for all to see.

Empty graves

In some parts of the world you can see standing stones, topped with horizontal ones. These were underground tombs, dug over 2,000 years ago. Since then, the earth over them has been worn away, exposing the stones.

Crater Lake in Oregon was formed about 7,000 years ago when Mt. Mazama erupted in a huge explosion and the sides of the mountain fell. The crater which it left gradually filled with water.

Dangerous women

There were four dangerous female creatures in mythology. **1** The Harpy had a woman's head and a bird's body. **2** The mermaid had a woman's body and a fish's tail. **3** The siren had a woman's body and a bird's wings and legs. **4** The sphinx had a woman's head and a lion's body.

Goalie's goal

A goalkeeper once kicked a ball from his own goal area the length of the entire soccer field. It bounced into the opponent's goal!

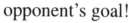

When you are born, you have more than 800 bones in your body. By the time you are grown, you have only 206 bones. Some of your bones, including some that make up your skull, join together as you grow.

Ant herders

Some ants keep herds of aphids – tiny insects that live on plants – like people keep cows. The ants protect and look after the aphids. They "milk" them by stroking them with their antennae. The aphids then produce drops of clear liquid, which the ants quickly lick up.

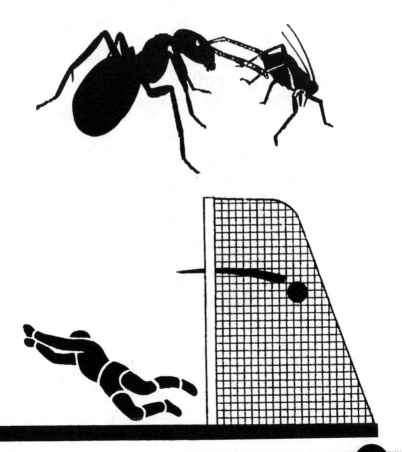

Billions of snowflakes fall on the ground every year, but each one is different. Snowflakes are made of tiny ice crystals which freeze together in the clouds. Most of them have six sides.

Crying wolf
If you had a mental illness called lycanthropy, you would think you were a wolf.

The footprints left by astronauts walking on the Moon will still be there in a million years. There is no wind, rain, or water on the Moon to wash or blow the footprints away.

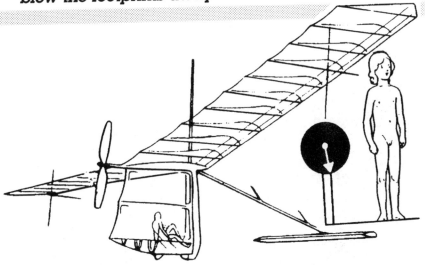

Pedaling high
An American cyclist, Bryan Allan, pedaled into the sky on a self-propelled glider-bike. It weighed only 70 lb (32kg) – the weight of a ten-year-old child.

Moving stage
The landlord of the Globe Theatre in Britain, where William Shakespeare and his friends acted nearly 400 years ago, raised the rent. The actors took down the building and put it up on another site.

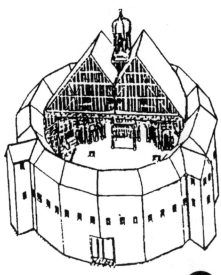

Fulmars protect their nests by spitting an oil at any predator that comes near. The oil is made in the bird's stomach from the food it eats, and it smells terrible.

Holes in the head

If something goes wrong inside your head and a surgeon has to operate on part of your brain, she first cuts a flap of skin to reveal your skull. Then she drills five holes in your skull and cuts around the holes with a saw. She lifts off the cut bone to get at your brain. When the operation is over, she reattaches the piece of bone and sews back the flap of skin. Of course, you are unconscious during the operation.

Tiny ant

Some ants are so tiny, they could fit inside this letter o.

The Amazon River is the second largest river in the world. One-fifth of all the world's river water flows out of its mouth into the Atlantic Ocean. Starting as a stream in Peru, it is nearly 4,000 miles (6,437km) long.

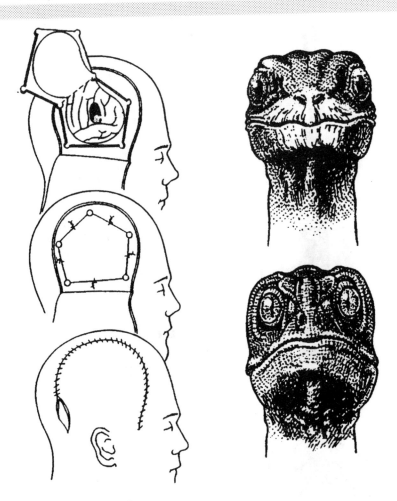

Watch out!

A dinosaur with eyes on the sides of its head, like a horse, could see an enemy coming from the side or even from behind. A dinosaur with eyes on the front of its head could only see forwards. These were the ones that chased and ate other creatures.

Some plants spread their seeds by using animal or bird carriers. When an animal or bird brushes against the plant, the seeds stick to their fur or feathers. The seeds drop or are rubbed off miles away.

Channel tunnel

The first plan for a tunnel between Britain and France was conceived by the French emperor Napoleon Bonaparte nearly 200 years ago. Nothing was done until 1875, when digging began on the French side. This was stopped because British generals feared it could be used by the French to invade England. The present tunnel was completed in 1993 and opened in 1994.

Sheepskin or chamois leather?

Real chamois leathers are made from the skin of "goat antelope" or "chamois." A lot of leather cloths you wash cars with are really made from sheepskin.

The world's longest mountain range is mostly underwater. The Mid-Atlantic Ridge is 9,942 miles (15,997km) long and stretches all the way from the north Atlantic Ocean to the Antarctic.

Money bird

Male quetzal birds have beautiful long tail feathers which were once worn by ancient Mayan chiefs as a symbol of authority. Now the bird is Guatemala's national symbol, and the country's money is named after it.

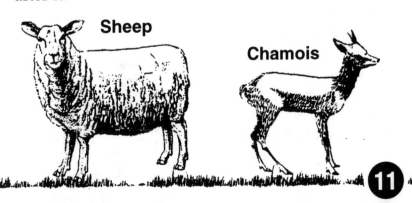

Sheep

Chamois

There are about 250,000 different types of flowers in the world – and that's not counting all the flowers that have been specially grown for their size, color, and scent.

Misplaced

Can you see the fish, a plaice, in this picture? Some fish are able to change the pattern and color of their skins to match the sea floor on which they lie.

Safe on high

American inventor Elisha Otis built the first safety elevator in 1852. Such elevators allowed builders to construct very tall buildings.

Some spiders are big enough to eat birds. They live under logs and in holes in the ground in forests in South America, Africa, and Asia. Their bodies are as big as oranges and their legs as long as pens.

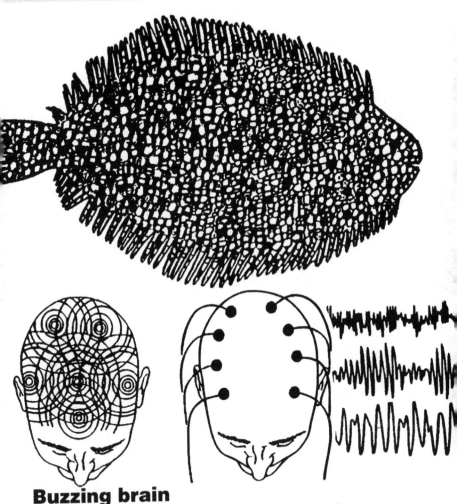

Buzzing brain

Your brain gives off tiny electrical signals. Electrodes attached to your head can pick up these signals and record them on a machine. These "brain waves" show how you react to various things and what condition your brain is in.

The River Ganges is sacred to the Hindus of India. The riverbanks are lined with temples, and steps – called ghats – lead down to the water. Every year thousands of Hindu pilgrims go to bathe in the river.

Helpful hands

A shrimp has nineteen pairs of arms or legs. You have only two pairs. It uses two pairs to find food in the water, one pair as jaws, five pairs to handle the food, five pairs to walk with, five pairs to swim and breed, and the last pair as a tail.

Animal weed killer

Manatees are used in Guyana to keep waterways clear of weeds. A fully grown manatee is 16 feet (4.9m) long and eats 100 lb (45kg) of weeds a day – about the same as 1,500 small bags of potato chips.

Human warble flies lay their eggs on female mosquitoes. When the mosquito lands on a human being to bite him, the warble fly eggs hatch, and the maggots burrow into the person's skin.

Roman frontier

For seven years, starting in AD 122, Roman soldiers worked to build a wall across northern England to keep out raiders from Scotland. It is called Hadrian's Wall, after the emperor who ordered it built. It had a rampart 15 feet (4.6m) high, with a deep ditch on the Scottish side, and forts at intervals. You can still walk along parts of it today.

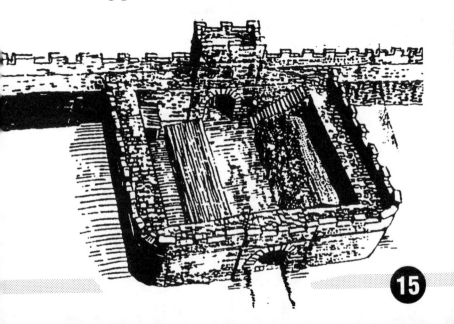

Mt. Etna, on the island of Sicily, is the highest active volcano in Europe. It has erupted 260 times since it was first recorded nearly 3,000 years ago. Liquid rock hums and roars inside the volcano.

Short life

A mouse lives for only two or three years – on average human beings live 25 times longer.

What a pile up!

An Australian bird called a mallee fowl makes the biggest nest in the world. First it scratches up a huge mound of plants. It lays its eggs in a hole in the center and then heaps more plants on top. As the plants rot, they heat up, keeping the eggs warm until they are ready to hatch. The bird opens the nest to cool it down during the day and covers it up at night.

Stegosaurus may have been the stupidest of all the dinosaurs. It had a big, heavy body that weighed up to 2 tons (1.8 metric tons), but its tiny brain weighed only about 2 ounces (56gm) – as much as one chicken's egg.

Young genius

The great composer Wolfgang Amadeus Mozart was writing piano pieces by the time he was five. He was only six years old when his father took him on a concert tour.

Wonder worm

The record length for a South African earthworm is 22 feet (6.7m) – the length of seven garden spades.

Your ears tell you if you are standing up, leaning over, or lying down. Special cells in tubes of liquid in your inner ear send messages about your movements to your brain. They help you to know what you are doing.

Half men

In ancient Greek mythology, there were creatures with a man's head, arms, and chest but with the bodies of animals. A centaur had the body and legs of a horse. A triton had a horse's front legs and a fish's tail.

Leopards store their food in trees, where it is safe from jackals and hyenas. After a leopard makes a kill, it feeds on the meat. Then it drags the remains of the animal up a tree and hangs them from a branch.

Mega spider
This is the actual size of the world's largest spider – the South American bird-eating spider.

Devil's Tower in Wyoming stands 869 feet (264.8m) above the Belle Fouche River. According to a Native American legend, the strange ridges down its sides were made by a giant bear trying to reach the people on the top.

Not a piggy

Tapirs, which live in Central and South America and Malaysia, look a little like pigs. But they do not belong to the pig family. Only about 3 feet (.9m) tall, they are related to horses and rhinos.

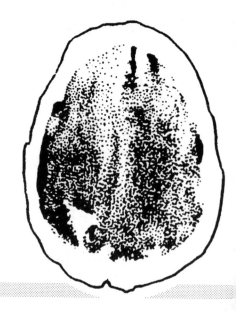

Cat's eye

The special method of using X rays called computerized axial tomography (CAT scan) was invented in 1973. Doctors use it to look at what is going on in a living body.

There are probably over 80 million different types of insects in the world. This is more than all the different types of animals and plants. And each type might include billions of insects.

Boneless fish
Manta rays, like other rays and sharks, have no bones. Their skeletons are made of tough cartilage or gristle.

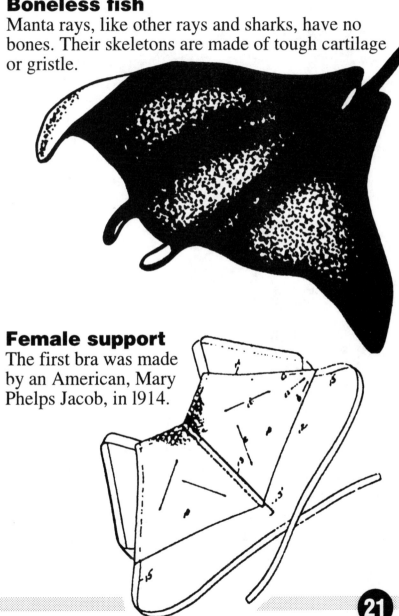

Female support
The first bra was made by an American, Mary Phelps Jacob, in 1914.

You have about five million hairs on your body. Many of them are so fine, you can hardly see them. They grow at an average rate of up to .5 inch (1.3cm) a month but a little faster when the weather is warm.

Short leg

Colin Jackson won a gold metal for Britain in the Olympic hurdle race in 1988. What few people knew was that he had a pad in his left shoe. This was because his left leg is .5 inch (1.3cm) shorter than his right leg.

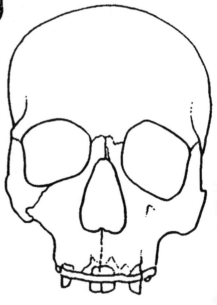

Old teeth for new?

The earliest known false teeth were worn by the Etruscans in central Italy about 3,000 years ago.

A housefly walks on the ceiling, clinging on with its six feet. On each foot are tiny tubes which act as suction pads. The tubes also release a sticky substance which helps the housefly walk on smooth surfaces.

Great Wall

The Great Wall of China is the biggest structure in the world. It runs across northern China for 2,162 miles (3,480km), with branches and spurs almost that long. It was built more than 2,000 years ago to keep out raiders from the north.

Loud howler

Howler monkeys live in the tropical forests of South America. They howl at dawn, when two groups meet, and when they are disturbed. Their roars can be heard nearly 2 miles (3.2km) away.

Greenland is the largest island in the world. Most of the land is covered with sheets of ice. The temperature is usually below freezing, and it snows all year round.

Mother tongue
The mother of Joseph Stalin, former leader of Communist Russia, never learned to speak the Russian language.

Getting at it
Some birds drop stones onto other birds' eggs to crack them open. Then they eat them. Gulls drop crabs from a height to break open the shells. A woodpecker finch pushes a sharp stick into cracks in trees to pick out grubs and insects.

The stars you can see on a clear night are part of our galaxy, the Milky Way. It is so big that if you drove a fast car across it, the journey would take about 665,000 million years.

Tuned in

Some scientists think that there are people who can read minds and "see" what others are thinking.

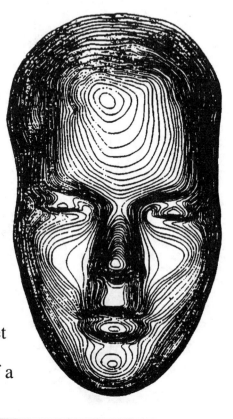

Field landing

A jumbo jet is 195 feet (59.3m) long – well over half the length of a soccer field.

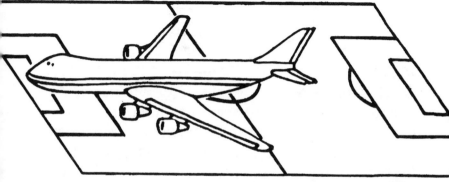

About 10 million free-tailed bats are born each year in Bracken Cave in Texas. The babies hang onto the walls of the cave while their mothers go out to find food. Each mother always manages to find her own baby.

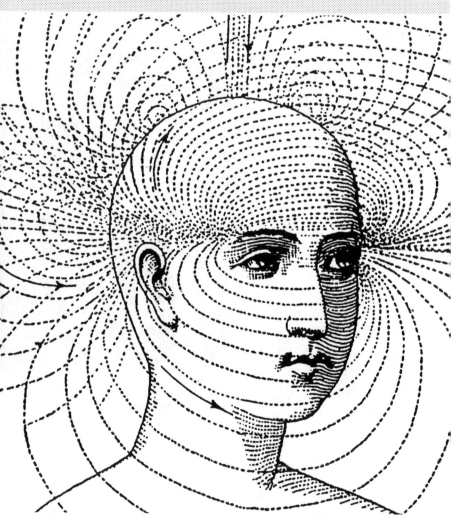

Sixth sense

Human beings have five senses – touch, sight, hearing, taste, and smell. Some people believe we have a sixth sense that alerts us to danger and that gives us glimpses of the future.

One of the world's most poisonous creatures is a type of jellyfish called a sea wasp. It lives in the Pacific Ocean. After being stung by a sea wasp, a swimmer sweats, goes blind, cannot breathe, and dies in a few minutes.

Mother's boy

The gangster Al Capone could not talk to his mother when she visited him in prison. Only English was allowed, and she spoke only Italian.

Pickled!

British admiral Horatio Lord Nelson was wounded at the Battle of Trafalgar against the French in 1805. He died on his ship *Victory*. To stop his body from decomposing on the long journey back to England, it was put into a barrel of brandy.

When Mt. St. Helens, in Washington state, exploded in 1986, 1,300 feet (396m) blasted off the top of the volcano. Hot gas, steam, ash, and rocks shot out, killing millions of birds, animals, and fish.

Winning by a beak
In South Africa, jockeys wearing full racing colors race on ostriches.

Long life
The oldest recorded tortoise was 152 years old – that is twice the average life span of most human beings.

An orangutan, a very large ape, builds a nest in the trees every night. It makes a mattress out of bent branches in the fork of a tree and covers itself with a blanket of leaves, all in about five minutes.

Shocking treatment

Some scientists believe that when a person is hypnotized, an electrical magnetic force is transmitted by the hypnotist.

Bird snatcher

The ancient Greeks believed there were women with birds' bodies called Harpies. They stole food from their victims.

Super snail

This is the actual size of the head of the world's largest snail. It lives in Africa, and it is four times as long as the width of this page.

The Sun is a star that you can see during the day. It is a very hot ball of hydrogen gas. It uses up about 4 million tons (3.6 million metric tons) of gas every second but it has enough to keep going for another 5,000 million years.

Grave error

The painter Vincent van Gogh was named after a brother who had died at birth. All Vincent's life, there was a grave with his name on it.

Big blast

In 1783, a volcano erupted in Iceland. It released a huge cloud of dust and gas which caused the deaths of 10,500 people and floated for months over Europe.

In only a few square miles (sq km) of rain forest there may be 700 kinds of trees, 1,000 different flowering plants, 450 different kinds of birds, 100 different animals, and 100 types of moths and butterflies.

Long walk

Captain Scott and his team of explorers walked 950 miles (1,528km) from the Antarctic coast to the South Pole. On their return, they ran into trouble and all died. If they had succeeded, their journey would have been the same as walking from London to Moscow in temperatures well below zero.

Below the line

Every merchant ship has a line on its side, showing the level it can sink to when safely loaded. It is called the Plimsoll line, after Samuel Plimsoll, a British Member of Parliament, who campaigned against the danger of overloading ships.

Flamingos get their orange-pink color from their food. They eat shrimps and tiny water plants that contain an orange substance called carotene. Without this food, their feathers slowly turn a dull gray.

Not a part of a bird

A dovetail is a way of joining two pieces of wood. Their ends are cut into special interlocking shapes.

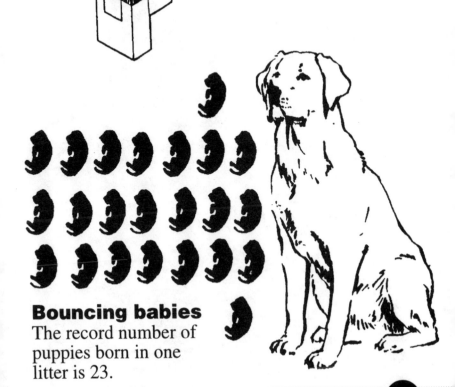

Bouncing babies

The record number of puppies born in one litter is 23.

A Portuguese man-of-war jellyfish has tentacles up to 65 feet (19.8m) long. They are covered with spines which shoot poison into anything that touches them. The poison kills fish and is very painful to people.

Night sight
Modern soldiers have special telescopes fitted to their rifles so they can see in the dark.

Long flier
Painted lady butterflies fly from North Africa to Iceland.

Glyphs for numbers
Ancient Mayans in Mexico used pictographs to represent numbers.

1　**2**　**3**　**4**　**5**　**10**

In 1955, red snow fell on the Alps in Europe. The snow was colored by dust which had been carried by winds from the Sahara desert in North Africa, over 1,800 miles (2,895km) away.

Pining away

A pineapple does not grow on a pine tree and is not an apple. It got its name because it looks like a pine cone.

Quick march

You can easily tell a centipede from a millipede – centipedes have four legs on each section of their bodies; millipedes have only two.

Wolves howl to tell each other where they are and to call the pack together at the end of a hunt. Sometimes the whole pack will howl. One starts, and the others join in. They can be heard more than 7 miles (11km) away.

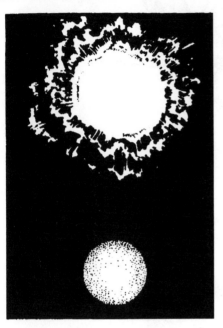

Age of the Earth

In 1654, Archbishop James Ussher of Ireland used the Bible to determine that Earth was created in 4004 BC. We now know that it is at least 4,600 million years old.

Quick families

The record number of baby mice born of one mother at one time is 34.

Adelie penguins spend the winters feeding far out at sea. In September and October, they go back to their nests on the ice and snow in the Antarctic. They can't fly, but they waddle up to 200 miles (322km) across the ice.

Reverse again

When you take a photograph, the image you capture is reversed in three ways. The top is at the bottom, the right is on the left, and the light areas appear dark.

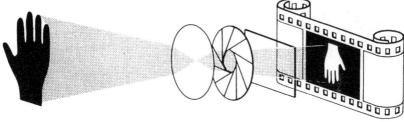

Largest number

Red-billed queleas are thought to be the most numerous birds in the world – there may be more than 10,000 million in Africa.

Six fingers

Anne Boleyn, the mother of Queen Elizabeth I of England, was born with six fingers on her right hand.

Outer space is not empty. There are lots of rocks, dust, pieces of meteorites, and comets. There are also used rockets, old and broken satellites, and even tools dropped by astronauts.

Lucky hand

You get just one combination out of 2.5 million when you are dealt five cards from a 52-card deck.

Male or female

You can tell male from female earwigs by the shape of their pincers. A male has curved ones, and a female has straight ones.

Beavers can cut up a log 20 inches (.5m) thick with their sharp teeth in just 15 minutes. They cut down trees to make a dam and then build their home, called a lodge, in the pond which forms behind the dam.

Useful neighbors

Birds called yellow-rumped caciques build their nests next to wasps' nests in South America. Most animals will not disturb a wasps' nest. So the caciques' nests are protected by their stinging neighbors.

Riding on air

The air-filled bicycle tire was invented twice. The first inventor was a Scot, Robert Thomson, but he did not develop it. Another Scot, John Dunlop, began manufacturing his air-filled tire more than 100 years ago.

The world's greatest travellers are Arctic terns. Each year, these birds fly all the way from the Arctic to the Antarctic and back again – a round trip of more than 25,000 miles (40,225km).

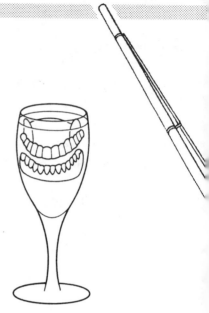

Chew on this

George Washington had several sets of false teeth. They were made from elephant tusks, lead, and cow, hippo, and human teeth. It is said he soaked his false teeth in wine each night to make them taste good.

Stinging tale

Scorpions were the first animals in the world to live on land. They have been around for 440 million years.

Tall buildings sway and bridges tremble in gale-force winds. The bridge over the Tacoma Narrows in Washington state shook so much it was called "Galloping Gertie." It eventually fell down in a violent storm.

A smasher!

Birds can be very clever at getting the food they want. A thrush smashes a snail's shell against a stone to get at the flesh inside.

Paris gun

This huge gun was used by the German army to shell the city of Paris at a distance of 74.5 miles (120km) in World War I.

A Canadian porcupine has over 30,000 quills on its body. If it is attacked, it backs into its enemy, pushing in its needle-sharp quills. Then it walks away, leaving a few quills behind.

Rain rattles

The Hopi Indians of the southwestern United States used to try to make it rain in their desert area. They danced around with rattlesnakes in their mouths, pleading with the rain gods to send them showers.

Golden nose

Tycho Brahe, the famous astronomer, had part of his nose cut off in a sword fight. He had a false nose made of gold, silver, and wax. It was painted to look like skin. He wore it for 30 years, until he died in 1601.

Have a banana!

Ancient Greeks, Romans, and Arabs ate bananas. Early explorers took them across the Atlantic to the Caribbean islands.

The world's biggest clamshell is more than 3 feet (.9m) across. Stories that fishermen's feet have been trapped by the clam are not true. Its shell closes so slowly, they have plenty of time to escape.

Ancient insects

Over 280 million years ago, giant insects like dragonflies lived on Earth. This was long before there were dinosaurs. You can see their descendants hovering over ponds and streams.

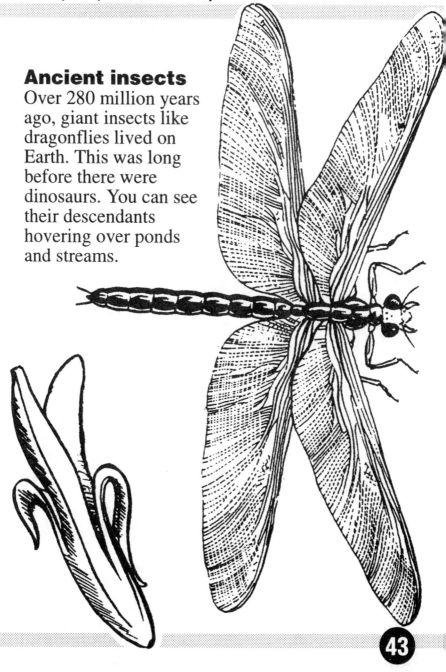

The wandering albatross has the longest wings in the world. They are up to 12 feet (3.6m) from wing tip to wing tip. This bird flies over 500 miles (804km) a day across the south Indian Ocean, using the air currents.

Slow mummy

It took the ancient Egyptians ten weeks to prepare a dead body and wrap it, before putting it in a coffin.

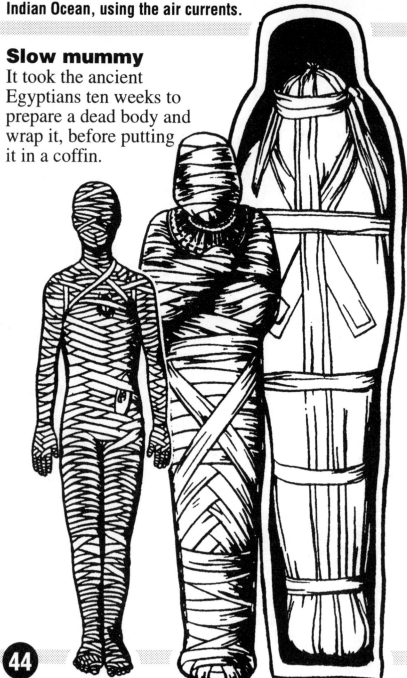

Humpback whales catch fish in a net of bubbles. A whale swims under the fish and squirts out a circle of bubbles from its blowhole. The fish stay inside the circle, and the whale then swallows them.

Love apples

Tomatoes were once called love apples because people thought they inspired love. They were grown for food by Native Americans long before Columbus arrived.

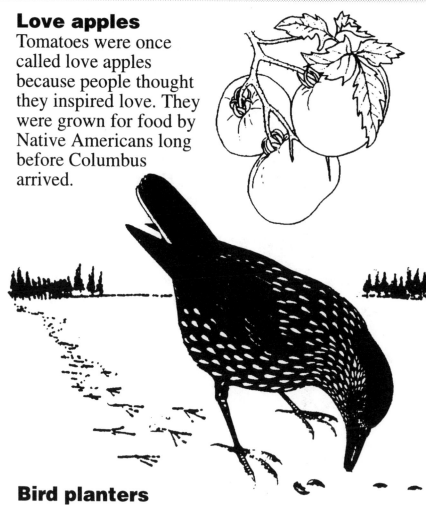

Bird planters

Thick-billed nutcracker birds, native to Scandinavia, hide stores of nuts to eat during the winter. Although a bird remembers where it buried the nuts, it sometimes misses a few. These grow into trees, helping the forest to spread.

Crows make about 300 different sounds to call to each other and to warn off enemies. Crows live in many parts of the world, and, like people, they have different languages in different countries.

Glittering gold

Gold does not tarnish or corrode but stays bright forever. It is a very soft metal and can be hammered into any shape.

Anting

Some birds use ants to clean them. They sit with their feathers fluffed up and let the ants crawl over them. The ants squirt out an acid which kills the insects living on the birds.

The loneliest people in the world are the 300 or so who live on Tristan da Cunha in the Atlantic. This is the most isolated inhabited island on Earth. Their nearest neighbors are 1,320 miles (2,124km) away.

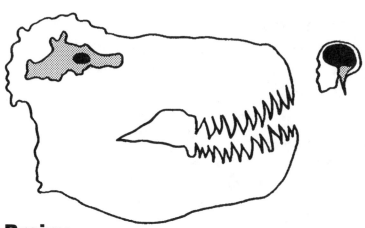

Brainy

Although the brain (the gray area) of the dinosaur Tyrannosaurus was bigger than a human's, the thinking part – the black area – was much smaller.

Bugs alive

This is not a monster but a tiny bug, only 1 mm long. It can live on your body, biting and sucking your blood. It's called a crab louse.

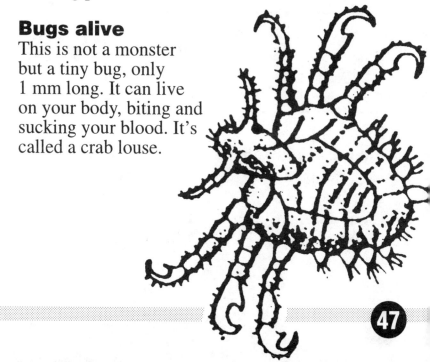

Mudskippers use their fins to skip over the mud of mangrove swamps in Southeast Asia. These strange fish can breathe through their skin when out of the water and through their gills when they are in the water.

Leaping lions

Lions are shown on badges, coins, flags, and stamps. There is a special name for each way a lion leaps, stands, sits, or lies.

1 Lion rampant
2 Lion statant guardant
3 Lion rampant
 guardant
4 Lion passant
5 Lion statant
6 Lion passant
 guardant

7 Lion sejant
8 Lion sejant rampant
9 Lion couchant
10 Lion salient
11 Lion coward
12 Lion queue fourchée

Thousands of mammoths have been found frozen in the ice in Siberia in Russia. Looking like big wooly elephants with long curved tusks, these animals died between about 25,000 and 40,000 years ago.

So many cells

The back of your eye is called the retina. Although it is quite small, it contains 137 million cells. It has 130 million cells to help you see black and white, and 7 million cells to help you see colors.

This is the actual size of your retina.

Mini molecules

A molecule is a tiny piece of something, so small you can only see one with a powerful microscope. Molecules are so tiny that one spoon of water contains as many molecules as there are spoons of water in the Atlantic.

The male bellbird is one of the loudest birds. Sounding like a clanging bell, it can be heard over half a mile (.8km) away. It sings to attract a mate. When a female comes close, it dances out and sings again.

Typecast

Over 100 years ago, some scientists believed that the shape of your head showed the type of personality you had. Are any of your friends' heads shaped like one of these?

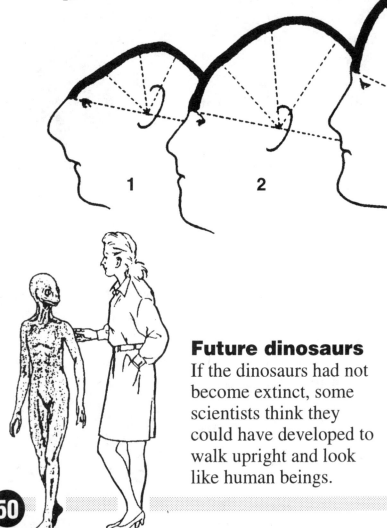

Future dinosaurs

If the dinosaurs had not become extinct, some scientists think they could have developed to walk upright and look like human beings.

Oil is processed to make fuel for cars. It is also used to make medicines, explosives, pesticides, detergents, glues, polishes, paints, nylon, plastics, and even makeup.

1 Idiot
2 Criminal
3 Poet or thinker

4 Likely to commit crimes
5 Likely to be honest

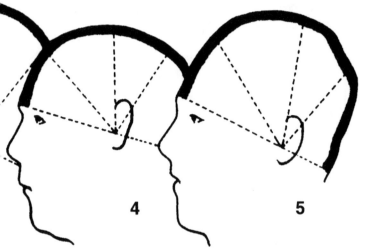

4   **5**

Startling eyes

When this moth has its wings folded, it looks like a piece of old bark. If a bird comes near, it opens its wings and shows two spots that look like eyes. The startled bird is likely to fly off without trying to peck at the moth.

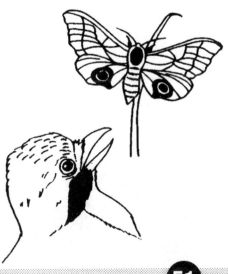

African baobab trees have very fat trunks which they use to store water. The trunks of some old baobabs are hollow and have been made into bus shelters and even homes for people to live in.

Box gogglers

It is estimated that by the time you are 18 years old, you will have watched more than 15,000 murders on television and seen more than 360,000 commercials.
In all, you will have spent 17,000 hours in front of the box.

Royal palace

A great palace was built at Versailles, outside Paris, in the seventeenth century for the French king Louis XIV. It had a Hall of Mirrors 240 feet (73m) long, lit by 3,000 candles. In the gardens were 1,400 fountains. The palace was open to the public, and people could wander through its rooms and even watch royal births.

The oldest known clothes are about 37,000 years old. They were found on the body of a man frozen in the ground in Siberia. Made of animal skins, they were sewn together with strips of leather.

What a corker!

Table tennis was invented by James Gibb over 100 years ago. It was first played with paddles made from cigar-box lids and champagne corks for balls. The game is also called Ping-Pong™.

Walking on water

A South American lizard can walk on water, but not for very long. It has powerful back legs and broad feet with fringed toes that keep it afloat. When scared by a predator, the lizard leaps from the riverbank and dashes across the water for as long as it can. Once it sinks, it can stay underwater for up to two minutes.

Diplodocus was one of the longest dinosaurs to have lived on the Earth. It was about 85 feet (25.9m) long, with a neck about 25 feet (7.6m) long. Although it was so big, it ate only leaves and plants.

Whose side are you on?

The pages of this book each have two sides. Turn over and look at the back of this one. You can make a strip of paper that has only one side. You don't believe it? Take a strip of paper. Twist it once and glue the ends together. Now try to color only one side of the whole strip.

Pedal power

A bicycle, ridden by three men and mounted on canoes, traveled down the River Thames from Oxford to London in Britain faster than an ordinary boat rowed by three men.

Outnumbered

There are more than 4,000 different types of mammal, including human beings. But there are more than 23,000 different types of fish.

A male Adelie penguin finds a mate by dropping a rock in front of another Adelie penguin. If the bird is female, she bows, and they mate. If it is male, it pecks the other male very hard.

riendly foe

orillas in zoos eat
eat. Those in the
ild eat only
uit and
egetables.

*The biggest eggs were laid by the elephant bird. They were over seven
times bigger than an ostrich's egg and weighed about 22 lb (10kg).
This extinct bird, which looked like a large emu, lived in
Madagascar.*

Sinking city

Mexico City is built on an underground reservoir.
Each year, the number of people in the city grows,
and more water is taken out of the reservoir. As a
result, the city is slowly sinking at a rate of about
6–8 inches (15–20cm) a year. This picture shows
the city in the middle of a lake at the time when
Europeans first explored America.

Geysers appear when water is heated by hot underground rocks in volcanic areas. There are more than 10,000 geysers at Yellowstone Park. Old Faithful geyser spouts 130 feet (39.6m) into the air every 30 to 90 minutes.

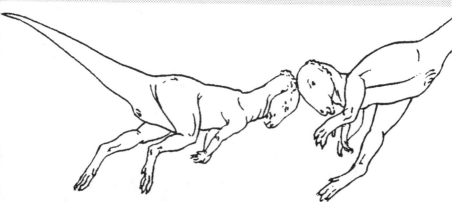

Head-bangers

Some dinosaurs fought for food or for mates by charging at each other and banging heads. Called "boneheads," they had thick skulls to protect their brains.

Sowing seeds

This bracket fungus, a type of mushroom, sheds its seeds, called spores, at a rate of 30,000 million a day for six months.

Manta rays are as big as a small plane, with "wings" up to 21 feet (6.4m) across. They flap their wings to swim slowly through the sea. Although they look scary, they are harmless and feed only on tiny sea creatures.

Talking trees

Scientists have discovered that trees may be able to talk to each other using a chemical language. When one tree is attacked by caterpillars which feed on its leaves, it sends out chemical signals to other trees. The trees' leaves make substances that the pests dislike, and this prevents the caterpillars from spreading to the other trees and eating them, too.

The Gulf Stream speeds across the Atlantic Ocean, bringing mild weather to Europe. New York is only 100 miles (160km) north of Lisbon in Portugal, but when it is freezing in New York, it can be quite warm in Lisbon.

Always in touch

Every part of your body is connected by nerves to your brain. The smallest change in temperature or softest touch sends a message to your brain, asking for action.

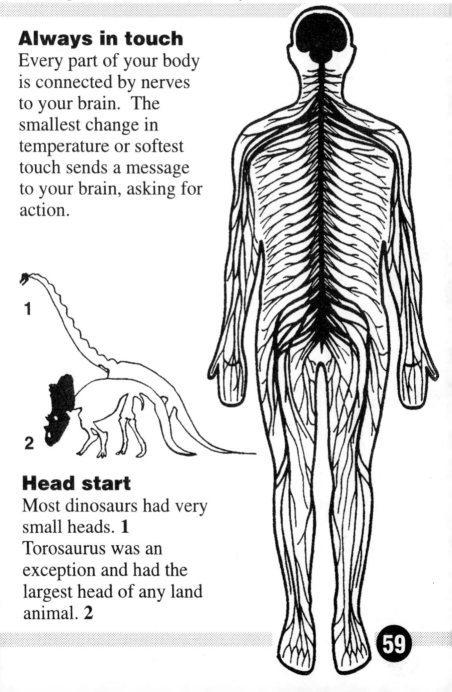

Head start

Most dinosaurs had very small heads. **1** Torosaurus was an exception and had the largest head of any land animal. **2**

Huge harpy eagles fly low over the rain forests of South America. Speeding through the tree tops, they use their claws to snatch monkeys, sloths, birds, and even porcupines to eat.

Skin tight

The ancient Mexican god of spring, Xipe Topec, wore a coat made of the skin of a sacrificed human.

Bigger billions

An American with a billion dollars has $1,000,000,000. A Briton with a billion pounds has £1,000,000,000,000. The European billion is 1,000 bigger than the American billion.

The first people to live in Australia sailed there about 30,000 years ago. They were the Aborigines, who crossed 40 miles (64km) of open sea from Indonesia and gradually spread all over the country.

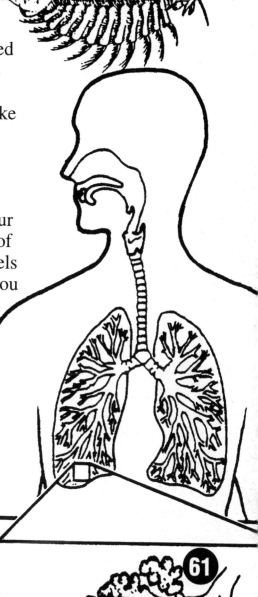

On its back

This tiny shrimp, called a brine shrimp, swims along upside down, moving its tiny legs like the oars of a rowing boat.

Lengthy lungs

Did you know that your lungs contain a mesh of very small blood vessels called capillaries? If you laid them out end to end, they would stretch for 1,500 miles (2,414km).

Pelicans have huge bags of skin under their beaks. They use them like nets to catch fish in the water. When their bags are full, the birds drain out the water. Then they toss their heads and swallow the fish whole.

Strong grass

Would you make furniture with grass? Some people do. Bamboo is a type of grass, the largest grass in the world. Its hard, woody stems are so tough they are used to make houses, chairs, tables, beds, flutes, and stakes for garden plants. There are more than 700 kinds of bamboo. Some grow up to 122 feet (37m) tall.

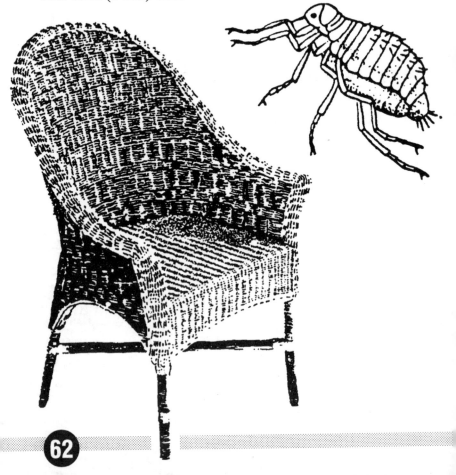

The biggest reef in the world is the Great Barrier Reef off the east coast of Australia. It is over 1,000 miles (1,609km) long. More than 400 different types of coral are busy building and repairing the reef.

Giant pearl

One of the largest pearls, the Pearl of Laotze, was found inside a giant clam. It was 9.5 inches (24cm) long and weighed as much as a three-month-old baby.

Killer fleas

A deadly disease, called the bubonic plague, killed more than a quarter of all the people in Europe in the fourteenth century. The disease was spread from rats to human beings by tiny biting fleas.

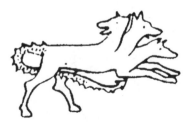

Guard dog

In ancient Greek mythology, the gates of the underworld were guarded by a dog with three heads, called Cerberus. It allowed only spirits of the dead to go in and let none out.

Every year gray whales swim from their feeding grounds in the Arctic to the coast of California, where they breed. They return when their calves are two months old – a round trip of about 13,000 miles (20,917km).

Colorful warning

The male anole displays his colorful throat flap to attract a female and warn off other males in the mating season. It is a member of the chameleon family.

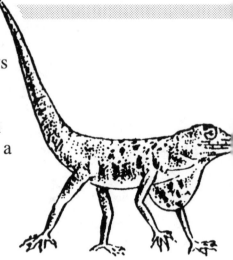

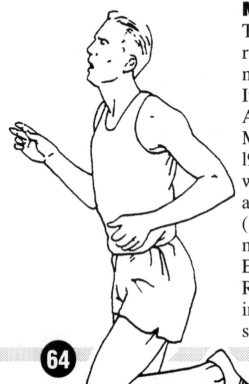

Milestones

The current record for running one mile is 3 minutes, 44.39 seconds. It was set by an Algerian, Noureddine Morceli, in 1993. Until 1954, people thought it was impossible for anyone to run a mile (1.6km) in under four minutes. In that year, an English medical student, Roger Bannister, ran it in 3 minutes, 59.4 seconds.

Bald eagles build the world's biggest nests. Each year the eagles use the same nest, adding more branches. A nest can be 9 feet (2.7m) across, 18 feet (5.4m) high, and weigh as much as a large car.

Single parents

Male and female jaguars live apart all the year and only meet during the mating season. The female gives birth to 2–4 young and brings them up on her own.

Old paper

The oldest surviving writing paper dates back to about AD 110 and was made in China.

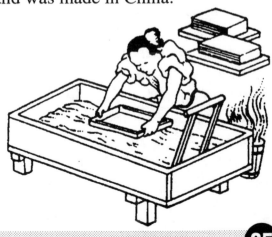

There are about one trillion (1,000,000,000,000) birds in the world. Over eight billion (8,000,000,000) of these are chickens reared for food. That is enough chickens for everyone in the world to have one and a half chickens each.

Superstition

Alberto Ascari won 20 Grand Prix races. He was so superstitious that he always drove wearing a lucky blue helmet and shirt. In 1955, he tried out a sports car without them and was killed.

Read all about it!

The first newspaper was printed in China about 1,300 years ago. It was called *Tching pao* – "News of the Capital." Another early government newspaper called *Acta Diurna* – "Daily Happenings" – was handed out free in ancient Rome.

The west side of a city is often a better place to live than the east side. In places with a temperate climate, the wind often blows from the west, bringing clean air and carrying smoke and dust eastwards.

Castle on a volcano

Edinburgh Castle in Scotland was built nearly 1,000 years ago on top of an old volcano. But there is no need to worry. The volcano, and another one nearby called Arthur's Seat, became extinct about 300 million years ago.

A green heron catches fish with bait. The bird drops an insect onto the water. Then it stands very still and waits. When a fish swims up to the bait, the heron spears its prey with its beak.

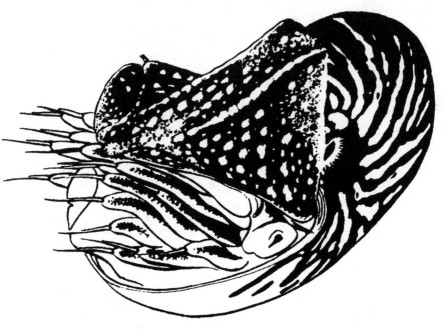

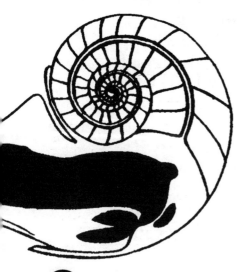

Moving house

A shellfish called a nautilus lives in a compartment in a coiled shell. As it grows, it moves out of the old compartment and builds a bigger one in front of it.

Nearly one-tenth of the world is covered with ice. The biggest ice sheets are in the Antarctic and in Greenland. The Antarctic ice sheet is one and a half times the size of the United States.

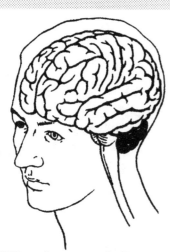

Wacky weights

An adult's brain weighs 3 lb (1.3kg), which is equal to the weight of three soccer balls.

Exploding balls

During World War II, the Germans dropped iron balls full of explosives (mines) into the sea. When a passing ship bumped into the floating ball and touched a point, the bomb exploded.

Niagara Falls will disappear in about 25,000 years. The river is very slowly wearing away the rocks on the edge of the Falls. About 10,000 years ago, the Falls were 7 miles (11.2km) downriver.

Getting around

Over 300 years ago, an English doctor, William Harvey, was the first to discover that your blood moves around your body. The blood in your big toe today may be in your ear tomorrow.

Not a home

Two-story stone houses built in the English Lake District were not for people. They were winter shelters for cattle.

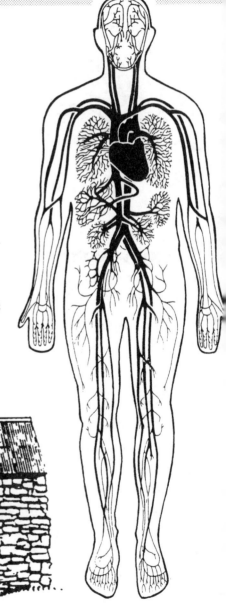

When the first cinema opened in Hong Kong, people had to be paid to go in. The Chinese believed the "moving spirits" on the screen had evil powers. But they soon got over their fears and paid to watch movies.

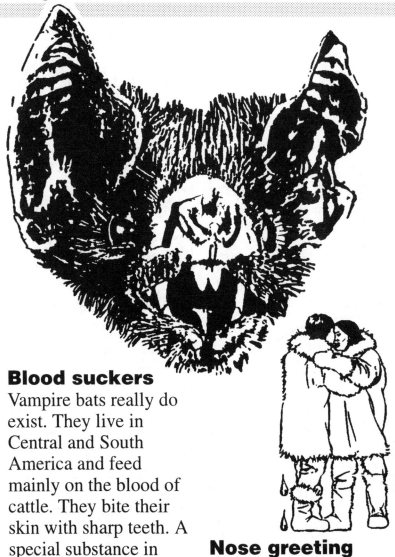

Blood suckers

Vampire bats really do exist. They live in Central and South America and feed mainly on the blood of cattle. They bite their skin with sharp teeth. A special substance in their saliva stops the blood from clotting while they lap it up.

Nose greeting

Eskimos say hello, goodbye, and kiss by rubbing noses.

Owls have huge eyes for hunting in the dark. Some can see fifty times better than a human being. An owl can't move its eyes to look to one side, but it can turn its whole head around to look backwards.

Good looker

Human beings' eyes face forward. They can see ahead and to each side. Fish, with eyes on the sides of their heads, can see behind them as well as in front.

In a thunderstorm, lightning and thunder happen at the same time. You see the lightning flash first and then hear the thunder because light travels faster than sound.

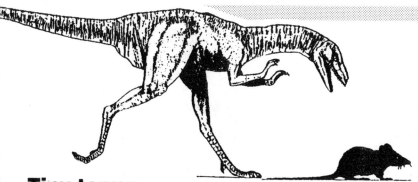

Tiny terror

Not all dinosaurs were huge monsters. This one, which lived about 150 million years ago, was only the size of a cat.

Back to front

No. 10 Downing Street, the official home of the British prime minister, is back to front. The famous front door is really the back entrance to two houses which are now joined into one.

"Mysterious dogs"

Native Americans caught and rode horses first brought to North America by Europeans. The Indians called them "mysterious dogs."

Yellowfin tuna are the fastest fish in the sea. When they see, hear, or smell their fishy food, they can reach a top speed of 45 mph (72km/ph) in a second. If they stop swimming, they sink slowly to the bottom.

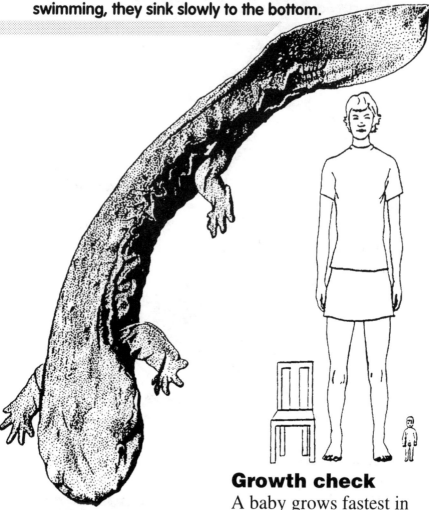

Pet monster
The hellbender is a giant salamander, about 30 inches (76cm) long. When kept as a pet, it will eat dog food.

Growth check
A baby grows fastest in the last three months before it is born. If it continued to grow at that rate it would be 18 feet 4 inches (5.6m) tall by 10 years of age.

All the cereals we eat and feed to animals have been developed over hundreds of years from wild grasses. They include wheat, corn, rice, oats, barley, millet, rye, and sorghum.

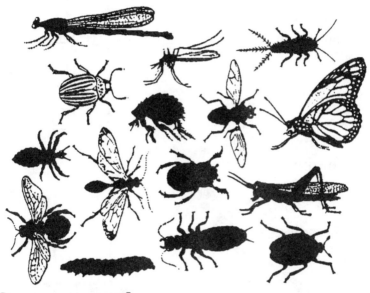

Creepy-crawly

Of all the different species of animal on Earth, nearly half of them are insects – there are over 950,000 different kinds.

Satchmo

Louis Armstrong, the great American jazz musician, learned to play the trumpet while he was in an orphanage in New Orleans.

Trumpeter swans take off from the water like a plane on a runway. To build up enough speed to get into the air, these heavy birds flap their wings and run across the water until they are airborne.

High divers

Professional divers in Acapulco in Mexico dive into water from rocks 118 feet (36m) high – equal to diving from the roof of an 11-story building.

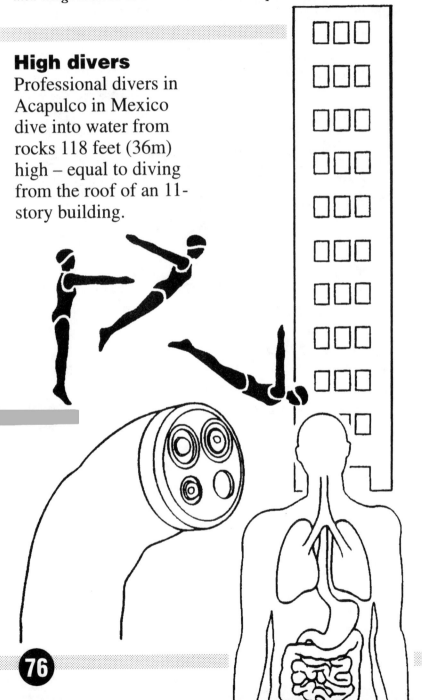

Waves wear away the coasts all the time. At Martha's Vineyard in Massachusetts, the cliffs are being worn away at a rate of about 5 feet (1.5m) a year. The lighthouse there has been moved inland three times.

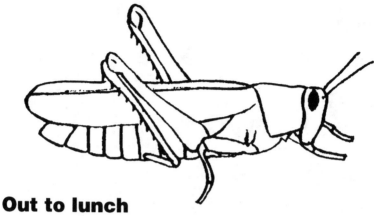

Out to lunch

A swarm of North African locusts can be so big it forms a black cloud which blocks out the Sun. A single swarm may have over 50,000 million locusts in it and cover 400 sq miles (1,036sq km). A swarm feeds at dawn and dusk, eating 3,000 tons (2,721 metric tons) of plants every day.

Inside view

Doctors can now look inside your body without having to cut you open. They insert a very thin fiber-optic tube. At the end of the tube are a light and a tiny camera. The camera sends back pictures so the doctors can see what is wrong with you and if you need surgery.

The tallest clouds are the great towering thunder clouds, called cumulonimbus. They can be twice the height of Mount Everest, the tallest mountain in the world, and hold 500,000 tons (453,500 metric tons) of water.

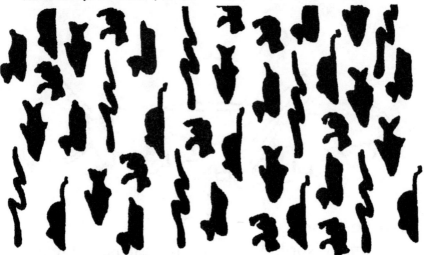

From out of the sky

There have been many reports of animals and fish falling out of the sky. No one knows how they get up there, although some people think they are swept up by strong winds. Here are some examples.

1 Bergen, Norway, 1578. Yellow mice fell into the sea and then swam ashore.

2 Singapore, 1861. After an earthquake, fish fell on the streets and bucketfuls were picked up.

3 Tennessee, USA, 1877. Thousands of snakes dropped out of the sky during a rain storm.

4 Birmingham, Britain, 1954. Hundreds of frogs fell on people's heads and hopped around in the streets.

5 Maryland, USA, 1969. Hundreds of dead ducks dropped down onto the streets.

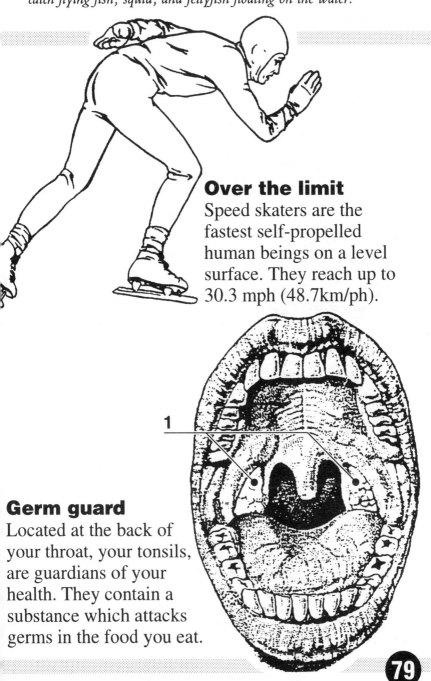

Frigate birds are the fastest of all the sea birds, with a top speed of 93 mph (150km/ph). They steal food from other birds while flying and catch flying fish, squid, and jellyfish floating on the water.

Over the limit

Speed skaters are the fastest self-propelled human beings on a level surface. They reach up to 30.3 mph (48.7km/ph).

1

Germ guard

Located at the back of your throat, your tonsils, are guardians of your health. They contain a substance which attacks germs in the food you eat.

The famous composer Beethoven began to go deaf when he was only 26. He was completely deaf when his Ninth Symphony was first performed in 1824. He helped the conductor keep time but could not hear the applause.

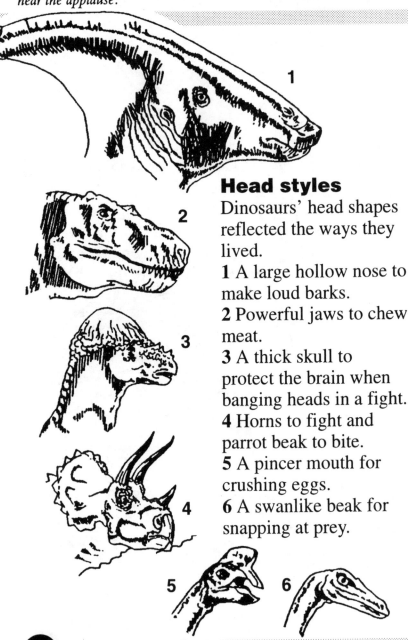

Head styles

Dinosaurs' head shapes reflected the ways they lived.

1 A large hollow nose to make loud barks.

2 Powerful jaws to chew meat.

3 A thick skull to protect the brain when banging heads in a fight.

4 Horns to fight and parrot beak to bite.

5 A pincer mouth for crushing eggs.

6 A swanlike beak for snapping at prey.

Saltwater crocodiles are the largest reptiles in the world. They grow up to 20 feet (6m) long. When a crocodile catches a big animal in its jaws, it turns over and over in the water to drown it before eating it.

Inside story

There are worms that live in animal and even human intestines. Some are tiny, but a tapeworm can grow up to 30 feet (9.1m) long.

Feather talk

Native Americans who lived on the plains wore feathers in their hair as a mark of victory over the enemy. The position of a feather and the paint on it carried messages, like these:

1 I was the third to wound the enemy in battle.
2 I killed three.
3 I cut his throat and scalped him.
4 I was wounded in battle.

Kiwis hunt for food at night using their noses. Most birds have noses at the base of their beaks, but kiwis' noses are at the tip. In the dark, they sniff out worms and insects to eat.

Getting the hump

There are two types of camel. A dromedary has one hump with a back like a D on its side. A Bactrian camel has two humps with a back like a B on its side.

Meatless monster

Adolf Hitler, the leader of the Germans during the 1930s and World War II, is said to have never eaten meat.

Sign of the times

The Chinese used a shadow clock to tell the time more than 4,500 years ago.

HITLER

Flying fish beat their tail fins from side to side and leap out of the sea at over 35 mph (56km/ph). They spread their side fins and glide through the air to escape from fish that are chasing them.

Fastest ever
Astronauts returning from the Moon in command module Apollo 10 in 1969 reached a speed of 24,791 mph (39,888km/ph).

Fossil clues
Fossilized evidence of dinosaurs includes:
1 footprint **2** droppings **3** print of skin **4** eggs

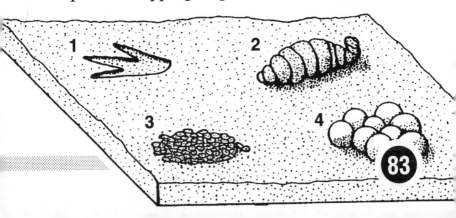

There were no sparrows or starlings in North America until about a hundred years ago when a New Yorker imported the birds. He wanted the United States to have all the birds named in Shakespeare's plays.

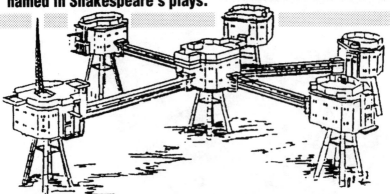

Moon station?

These castles on legs were built in Britain 50 years ago. Standing at the mouth of the River Thames, they guarded London from attack from the sea.

Junk box

The first television was made by John Logie Baird, a Scottish engineer, in 1924. He used cardboard, scrap wood, needles, and string for some of the parts.

You see a rainbow when the sun, shining on drops of water, is broken up into seven main colors. On the ground, you only see half a rainbow. In a plane, you see the whole circle of a rainbow.

Super Sun

Did you know that the Sun is 93 million miles (150 million km) from Earth? If you drove a car at 55 mph (88.5km), you would take 193 years to reach it. It is a ball of gas with a surface temperature of 2 million °C (3.6 million °F). Fountains of burning helium and hydrogen gas, called solar flares, shoot out from it into space.

Keeping warm

When you are asleep your body produces as much heat as a 100-watt lightbulb.

No people lived in North America until about 30,000 years ago. At that time, the sea levels were much lower, and hunters following herds could cross the Bering Strait on dry land from Asia.

Cockroach cure

About 2,000 years ago, a Greek doctor called Dioscorides Pedanius believed he had a cure for earache. All you had to do was scoop out a cockroach's stomach, mix it with oil, and stuff it in your ear. Later, another doctor said crushed cockroaches cured itching, swollen glands, and scabs. By the 1500s, cockroaches had spread all over the world and were a pest. Danish sailors earned a bottle of brandy if they killed 1,000 of them.

Guns into medals

Britain's highest military decoration for bravery is the Victoria Cross. Queen Victoria first awarded it in 1856, at the end of the Crimean War. For many years the crosses were made of bronze from Russian guns captured during the war.

More movies have been made featuring Sherlock Holmes than any other character in fiction. The famous detective, who always gets his man or woman, has been played by 68 actors in 187 movies.

Long story

Did you know that part of your food-processing system is a long tube called the small intestine, which is coiled up inside you? If you stretched it out, it would be 22 feet (6.7m) long. If you opened up all the tiny wrinkles in it, it would measure 360 sq yd (300.9 sq m).

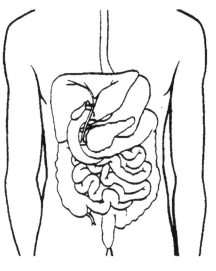

Whole new ball game

One of the world's most popular sports, so the story goes, was started by a British schoolboy. At Rugby School in 1823, William Webb Ellis was playing in a soccer game when he picked up the ball and ran with it. This was illegal, but it led to the start of a new ball game – rugby.

Seawater has a huge amount of salt dissolved in it. If all the salt could be taken out of the sea and spread over all the land in the world, it would cover the land with a layer of salt 500 feet (152.4m) thick.

Neck and neck

The longest neck of all, over 49 feet (14.9m) long, was that of the dinosaur Mamenchisaurus. It was over two-and-a-half times the height of a giraffe. Its neck had the same number of bones as a giraffe's neck.

Warrior queen

When the ancient Romans occupied Britain, Boudicca, the queen of an eastern tribe, rebelled. Her army attacked Roman towns and killed over 70,000 men, women, and children.

Every year, each person living in the United States uses things made from wood equal to one tree 100 feet (30.4m) tall. That comes to a forest of over 258 million trees in one year.

Cell-by date

The human body has about ten trillion cells. About three billion die every day and are replaced by new ones. The cells in your intestines last about three days, those in your liver about 18 months. Only the cells in your brain are never replaced.

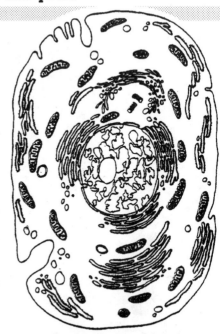

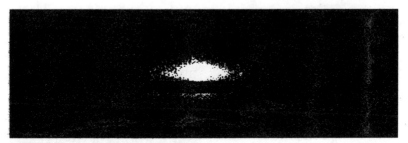

Light years away

Astronomers use the term "light years" to describe distances in space. There is a distant galaxy called 3C-295 which is 500 million light years away. What this really means is that it is 26,000,000,000,000,000,000,000 miles (41,800, 000,000,000,000,000,000 km) away from Earth!

Hurricanes were first given names by Clement Wragge, an Australian weatherman. Known as "Wet Wragge," he used the names of people he had quarrels with for the worst storms.

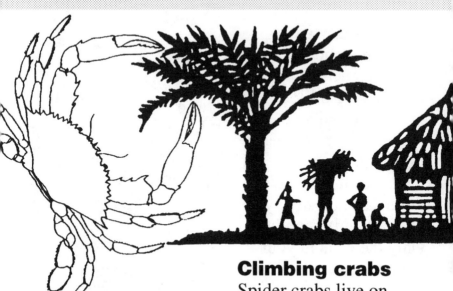

Climbing crabs

Spider crabs live on islands in the Pacific and Indian oceans. They grow to be about 18 inches (45.7cm) long and have very long legs, which they use to climb trees. When a crab gets to the top of a tree, it snips off a young coconut with its huge pincers and climbs down again to eat it.

Eye shadow

Ancient Egyptian women painted black eye makeup around their eyes. This helped to reduce the glare of the Sun.

Giant midgets

This is the actual size of an ant. Those in hot, wet areas of the world can be more than 1 inch (2.5cm) long.

Uncle Oscar

Every year, the Academy of Motion Picture Arts and Sciences awards a trophy to people who have made an outstanding contribution to cinema. The trophy – a golden statue – used to be called The Statuette. In 1931, Margaret Herrick spotted a copy of it and said, "Why, he looks just like my uncle Oscar." Since then, the awards ceremony and the statuettes have been called Oscars.

Forming fingers and toes

For the first 40 days of a baby's growth within the womb, it has no fingers or toes – only flippers. The fingers separate around the 50th day, and the toes form a week later. The little black shape above is the actual size of a 40-day-old embryo.

Twinkle twinkle little star

Stars may look as bright as each other, but this can be misleading. The star Alnilan (**A**) is 26,000 times brighter than our Sun, while Bellatrix (**B**) is only 2,000 times brighter than our Sun. Both look smaller because Alnilan is more than three times farther away from Earth (**C**).

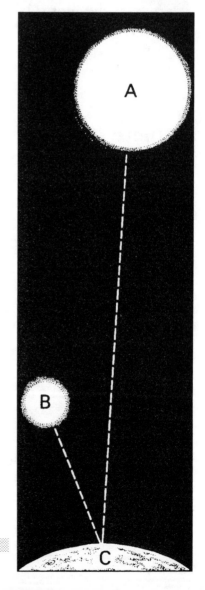

INDEX